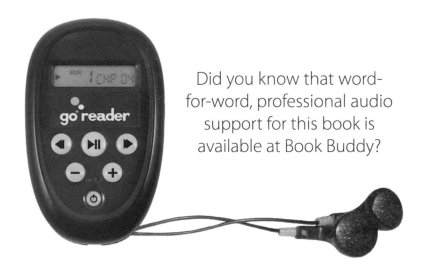

Did you know that word-for-word, professional audio support for this book is available at Book Buddy?

GoReader™ powered by Book Buddy is pre-loaded with word-for-word audio support to build strong readers and achieve Common Core standards.

The corresponding GoReader™ for this book can be found at: http://bookbuddyaudio.com

Or send an email to: info@bookbuddyaudio.com

YES *SHE* DID!

NEWS & MEDIA

Yes She Did! News & Media

Scobre Educational
2255 Calle Clara
La Jolla, CA 92037

Scobre Operations & Administration
42982 Osgood Road
Fremont, CA 94539

www.scobre.com
info@scobre.com

Scobre Educational publications may be purchased for educational, business, or sales promotional use.

Cover and layout design by Jana Ramsay
Copyedited by Renae Reed
Some photos by Getty Images

ISBN: 978-1-61570-944-1 (Soft Cover)
ISBN: 978-1-61570-943-4 (Library Bound)
ISBN: 978-1-61570-941-0 (eBook)

TABLE OF CONTENTS

CHAPTER 1
DOLLIES TO DIRECTORS

Imagine being a reporter during Martin Luther King, Jr.'s "I Have a Dream" speech. Or interviewing the first woman in America to vote. Or reporting from Vietnam with the war raging all around you. Marlene Sanders did all of this and more— and she was one of the first women to do it.

Women have been a part of the journalism world since the 1800s.

DARING TO DREAM

Just as Martin Luther King, Jr. had dreams of racial equality, female journalists in the 1960s dreamed of gender equality and were willing to work hard to achieve it.

However, for many years they were kept from working as professional journalists because of their gender. While a few women, such as Marlene Sanders, found their way to a professional career, the majority of women worked as secretaries and research assistants. The women who were hired as journalists weren't allowed to write. They would do the research for a story, then give it to their male counterparts to write. In the early days of journalism, these women were jokingly called "dollies" by their bosses. They were viewed as the pretty faces at the workplace, not as actual contributing members of the team. They were told that there would never be a real place for them in the world of media.

However, when the women's movement gained power in the 1960s, so did the dollies. The women working for *Newsweek* were the first to take a stand. With the help of one of the only female lawyers in practice, the 46 women employees of *Newsweek* were the first group of media professionals to sue their company for unfair treatment based on gender. When the *Newsweek* women took their story to the public on March 16, 1970, it quickly gained national attention and support. Only two days after their story went public, the ladies who worked at *Ladies' Home Journal* staged their own sit-in, and other groups quickly followed. Women in journalism refused to work until they were treated equally. Thanks to the work of the dollies, women were able to move up in the world of journalism. The few women who were already working as journalists, such as Marlene Sanders, were now able to move even higher, paving the way for others.

Marlene Sanders knew from an early age that she wanted to be in front of cameras. So, after a year of college, Sanders moved to New York to pursue a

DID YOU KNOW...

Marlene Sanders went to Ohio State University, where she majored in speech. However, she ran out of money and had to drop out after her first year.

career in acting. However, the theater was harder to break into than she anticipated. It wasn't working out as planned; so, in 1955 when Mike Wallace offered her a job at WNEW-TV, Sanders took it. As it turned out, it was the perfect fit.

At WNEW-TV, Sanders worked in a small unit, and was therefore expected to carry her weight. Unlike the dollies who were stuck pouring coffee, Sanders was learning how to dig for facts, edit, write, and produce. Sanders was a hard worker, and quickly moved up the WNEW-TV ranks. Mike Wallace saw her potential, and refused to let her gender keep her from being an asset to the company.

A BOOST FROM THE BEST

Mike Wallace was a journalist, media personality, and game show host during his career.

By 1962, Sanders was the assistant director of news—by far the highest position reached by any woman in the field. But Sanders pushed even higher.

In 1964, Sanders went to work as a New York correspondent for ABC News. At ABC, she got her biggest break—she became the first woman to anchor a nightly newscast for a major network. Sanders paved the way for women in journalism by proving that gender didn't matter. However, she wasn't alone in her fight. Many women, such as Jeannie Morris, were fighting to make their voices heard in the world of black and white.

ANOTHER FEMALE FIRST

Nellie Bly, another female journalism pioneer, was the first woman to go undercover, and in 1890, she set a record-breaking trip around the world.

CHAPTER 2
THE COLOR GIRLS

Sports reporters in the 1960s were not hard to identify: former professional athletes with good hair, big smiles, and a complete understanding of the game. So, when Jeannie Morris, the 5'2" wife of NFL wide receiver Johnny Morris, decided to join the world of sports reporting, everyone thought she was crazy; she definitely did not fit the profile.

Jeannie got her big break thanks to the help of her husband, Johnny. When he retired from the NFL, the *Chicago American* asked Johnny if he could write a newspaper column about football. He told them, "I can't. But my wife can."

DID YOU KNOW...

In 1971, Jeannie wrote a bestselling sports biography, "Brian Piccolo: A Short Season," the story of the Chicago Bears football player who died of cancer at 26. Jeannie turned all of her profits over to Piccolo's widow, Joy, and her three daughters.

Though they were skeptical, the *Chicago American* gave Jeannie her own column, called "Football is a Woman's Game" by Mrs. Johnny Morris. Though the column still possessed her husband's name, people quickly fell in love with football through the eyes of Jeannie.

In fact, Chicago loved Jeannie so much that she was offered a job at the *Chicago Daily News* as a sports reporter. Well, sort of. Although Jeannie was a sports reporter, she was never a "beat reporter," who reported the scores and statistics of the game. As a female, she wasn't allowed in the locker rooms and even in some press boxes so she couldn't talk directly to the players. Instead, Jeannie wrote interest pieces about the players, and gained popularity for herself, and the sport, by making the athletes come to life.

Jeannie then moved on to television, where she worked with some of the biggest stations in the

DID YOU KNOW...

Jeannie has interviewed many famous athletes, including NBA star Michael Jordan.

nation, including CBS. At CBS, Jeannie took many large steps towards women's equality. She was the first woman to interview players in the locker room, and in 1975, the first woman assigned to report live from the Super Bowl. However, when she showed up at the Super Bowl, she was told she was not allowed in the press box because she was a woman. But that didn't stop her. Instead, she did her report sitting on the top of the press box—in the middle of a blizzard!

MIXING WITH THE MEN

Though Jeannie was accepted as a sports reporter, she was not allowed in many of the press boxes because she was a woman.

However, while she found success in television, Jeannie eventually stepped down and retook her place as a newspaper columnist. According to Jeannie, "As a newsperson, I feel that your job is more informative and relevant." Jeannie's columns were still about sports, but her messages as a columnist were inspiring and universal. Though Jeannie has since left the world of journalism, her influence is still seen. Without Jeannie's work as a sports reporter, many women may not have gotten the opportunity to work in the sports world. And many women, such as Maureen Dowd, wouldn't have had the opportunity to become successful in the world of newspaper journalism.

Maureen Dowd began her career as a journalist in 1974, as an editorial assistant for *The Washington Star*. At *The Washington Star,* she took on numerous roles, including sports columnist, metropolitan reporter, and feature writer. In 1983, after

As the Washington correspondent, Maureen Dowd covered four presidential campaigns and elections.

making a name for herself, Maureen Dowd joined one of the most elite newspapers in the country: *The New York Times*.

In 1986, Dowd was named to be *The New York Times* Washington correspondent. She was only the second female to earn this position in the history of the paper. In her role, she quickly gained immense respect from politicians and journalists alike. Former President

13

George W. Bush humorously nicknamed Dowd "The Cobra," and she was frequently referred to as the "flame-haired flamethrower." Part of what made Dowd's articles so successful was that she didn't just focus on the politics at Washington; she focused on the politicians as well. In a teasing and somewhat informal manner, she made the politicians seem like real, approachable people.

In 1995, Dowd stepped down from her position as a Washington correspondent and became a *New York Times* op-ed columnist. Dowd's column primarily focuses on politics through the woman's perspective. She has declared herself part of "Team Color Girls." These are women in

newspapers who make a living writing about a male-dominated world.

Her pieces are humorous; they're like political cartoons depicted with words instead of pictures. She even tends to refer to her subjects by nicknames. For example, she called President Barack Obama "Spock" and "Barry." While her interest in the personality of politicians has earned her some criticism, she has continued to be immensely effective because she is not afraid to make jokes. She gets her point across in amusing, often unexpected ways.

However, Dowd's best quality is the fact that she never lets anyone forget that she's a woman. Unlike many other female journalists who write under male pseudonyms (false names), or from a male perspective, Dowd writes with the voice of a woman. By being proud of her gender, Dowd has given other women the courage to succeed. According to Leon Wieseltier,

Dowd's colleague, "she's the opposite of the woman who pulls the ladder up behind her. She keeps pushing it lower." Dowd's pride in her gender has given other women a ladder to climb the tower of success.

Maureen Dowd and Jeannie Morris are two extremely influential members of Team Color Girls. And while they are successful journalists, the highlight of their success is their ability, and willingness, to help other women like them succeed.

CHAPTER 3
BEHIND THE LENS

We have all seen pictures that have moved us to tears—pictures of baby elephants lying beside their dying moms, or starving children receiving food from Red Cross workers. Pictures that speak to us better than any written word. Pictures tell their own story—they bring information to life. Photography is an essential part of journalism, a profession in which many women have worked hard to succeed. Lynn Johnson and Jodi Cobb are two such women. While Jodi and Lynn could not be more different, they both achieved great success as photojournalists—journalists who tell a story through photography.

Lynn Johnson was a

DID YOU KNOW...

Photojournalism is a form of journalism. A photojournalist takes pictures, then edits and presents the images in order to tell a news story.

RISING ABOVE GENDER

shy girl growing up. She had a hard time connecting with the people around her, until the day she found photography. Lynn says that "when you're shy, a camera becomes an entry into life. It was a kind of shield I could hide my shyness behind, and it allowed me to become an active observer instead of a passive one." Once she bought her first camera, Lynn was hooked. Though photography was typically a profession for men, Lynn knew that it was where she was meant to be, and she wasn't going to let gender stereotypes stand in her way.

After majoring in photojournalism and photographic illustration at the Rochester Institute of Technology, Lynn got her first job with the *Pittsburgh Press*. Though she worked at the newspaper for seven years, she knew it wasn't what she truly wanted to do. Lynn believed that some of the stories needed more space than the newspaper allowed, and she wanted to work somewhere where she could give her subjects the recognition they deserved. So, Lynn decided to quit her job and become a freelance photographer. A freelance photographer is someone who works on their own, and is hired by many different companies to take pictures for them. As a freelancer, Lynn was hired to do journalistic photography for many popular magazines, such as *LIFE*, *National Geographic*, and *Sports Illustrated*.

Lynn strives to inspire change through her photography because "photographs help people look at things they may not want to look at. Until you can look at something, you can't change it." However, photography has not only helped Lynn to shape the world around her—it's also allowed her to shape herself. She's no longer the shy girl hiding behind the lens. Photography has allowed Lynn to talk to new people and to try new things—all activities that have helped her break free of her shell. She has photographed Tiger Woods, Stevie Wonder, and the U.S. Supreme Court. She has climbed to the top of the antennae on Chicago's Hancock Tower and dangled out of a helicopter in Antarctica. Lynn's life is an adventure—an adventure she wouldn't have been able to take without photography. And she's not the only one.

Jodi Cobb had a childhood very different

DID YOU KNOW...

As a freelance photographer, Lynn has been contracted to cover some of the most influential world events, including the 2004 Summer Olympics in Greece.

from Lynn Johnson. Jodi was an extremely outgoing, adventurous child. By the time she was 12, she had already been around the world twice, and spent a number of years living in Iran. Jodi was experiencing fabulous things, so she decided to start taking pictures of the people and places she saw. It was her adventurous spirit that led her to photography, and her spirit that

WOMEN OF VISION

Lynn (ninth) and Jodi (third) were both featured in National Geographic's "Women of Vision" Exhibition, which honored 11 extraordinary female photojournalists of the 21st century.

has allowed her to continue to succeed in the industry.

Jodi began her photography career taking pictures for newspapers but, like Lynn, she knew she wanted to do more. So when *National Geographic* offered her a job as their first female photographer, Jodi jumped at the chance to branch out in a new direction. At almost every job, Jodi has been the first female photographer there. Rather than be intimidated by the adversity, Jodi

TELLING THE TALE

Jodi took a six-month leave of absence from National Geographic *to work on her project*, Geisha: The Life, the Voices, the Art *(pictured below). The project took more than 3 years to complete.*

has found a way to make it an advantage.

Jodi's work focuses on many of the secret and unexplored societies around the world—societies where male journalists are not welcome. In 1987, Jodi was the first photographer to gain access into the hidden lives of women in Saudi Arabia. She produced a book, called *Geisha: The Life, the Voices, the Art*, which stepped into the lives of the geishas of Japan. Jodi knows that she's lucky to have the opportunity to pursue her career in photography, so much of her work focuses on women in other countries who are not so lucky. She hopes that by shining a light on human rights issues, such as gender inequality, she can help to change them.

Jodi's most famous piece was a *National Geographic* piece called "21st Century Slaves." It was a brutal look at human trafficking around the world, including in the United States. When we think of slavery, we think of something from history books. However, Jodi's piece proved that this is not the case—slavery and human trafficking is still happening today. The pictures were haunting, and told a story that no words ever could.

Through the project, Jodi traveled to 10 different

HEADLINE HERE

Jodi's advice to young photographers is that "there are stories everywhere—in your house, your backyard, your town. You just need to find out what you're interested in, what you want to change. It's right there—you simply need to get started."

countries and interviewed dozens of people directly related to the slave trade. When the project was published, it got the largest response of any article in *National Geographic* history. And the cool thing was, it wasn't just people congratulating Jodi on her work. People sent money to organizations that work to end slavery, and governments contacted Jodi to discuss ways to end slavery in their countries. The publication of the photographs actually instigated changes, just as Jodi had hoped it would.

Jodi and Lynn's work has opened up possibilities for other aspiring female photographers. Through their photography, both women have worked hard to gain gender equality around the world.

Photojournalism is an exciting career with endless stories to shoot, and wonderful opportunities for women behind the lens.

DID YOU KNOW...

After Jodi released "21st Century Slaves," the FBI asked to be trained in human trafficking issues because she had a better understanding about the problem in the United States.

CHAPTER 4
AIR TIME

The world of television news reporting is thrilling, and competitive. Many men and women dream of being the face of the news, yet only a few see any real air time. This has been especially true for women who have worked hard to gain the positions they deserve. One woman who has proven that hard-hitting journalism is a woman's job is Christiane Amanpour.

Christiane Amanpour had an amazing upbringing. She was raised in Tehran, Iran, but spent several years in a boarding school in London, England. No matter where she was though, Amanpour always dreamed of going to the United States. So, when she was given the opportunity, she went to the University of Rhode Island to study journalism. After graduation, she decided to stay in the U.S. and immediately looked for work.

CNN originally hired Amanpour as an entry-level desk assistant. She quickly proved, however, that she was capable of more than office work. She received her big break into television in 1986, when CNN asked her to cover the Iran-Iraq war. While critics

IN THE ACTION

Many places that Amanpour reports from are dangerous—she must wear protective gear and travel with military officers.

were initially worried that a woman wouldn't be able to handle the stress of being in such a dangerous situation, Amanpour knew better. Her successful reporting was off the charts, and CNN knew that they had found their newest reporter.

Amanpour's foreign reports brought her great recognition, while also taking the network to a new level of news coverage. She quickly found herself in the midst of exciting world events: she was in the middle of the democratic revolutions that swept Eastern Europe in 1989, and she had a front row seat to the Persian Gulf War. She even reported from Louisiana in the midst of

THE GLOBAL GIRL

Amanpour has reported from almost every hotspot around the globe and has interviewed almost every world leader.

Hurricane Katrina! With the hurricane raging around her, Amanpour bravely brought the disaster home for millions of Americans. In fact, she has been front and center in almost every major conflict and disaster in the last 30 years.

Amanpour has gained a reputation as a fearless and elite reporter. She also has a reputation for being honest. Amanpour has been criticized several times for failing to remain neutral during her reports abroad. To many people's surprise, she agrees. She told the critics that "there are some situations one simply cannot be neutral about, because when you are neutral you are an accomplice. Objectivity doesn't mean treating all sides equally. It means giving each side a hearing." Amanpour is considered one of today's leading news correspondents because she's not afraid to tell the American public what is really happening. She opens herself up to the criticism in order to tell the real story.

In recent years, Amanpour has proven that she's not only successful in the field—she's a great reporter in the newsroom too. Amanpour worked as CNN's chief international correspondent for almost 20 years. During her time with CNN, she interviewed some of the world's top leaders, including two Iranian presidents and the presidents of Afghanistan and Sudan. Not many people, men or women, can say that!

Amanpour made history again in 2011, when she began to work for two major networks simultaneously: CNN and ABC. She continued hosting a program on CNN International, while working at ABC News as a global affairs anchor.

Christiane Amanpour proved that women deserve their time on camera. Her hard-hitting reporting and bold personality allowed her to pave the way for female journalists everywhere. However, she

DID YOU KNOW...

Amanpour appeared on "Gilmore Girls," "Iron Man 2," and "The Pink Panther 2." Couric was the voice of "Katie Current" in the movie "A Shark Tale."

wasn't the only the woman making substantial strides in the news industry.

Katie Couric has long been called "America's Sweetheart" of television. However, like Amanpour, she didn't start out on camera. After graduating from the University of Virginia with a degree in American studies, Couric spent almost seven years working behind the scenes for various CNN bureaus around the country. When she got a job with NBC as a reporter in 1987, however, it was obvious to everyone that she had found a place where she belonged.

AMERICA'S SWEETHEART

"The Today Show" is a daily morning show that airs on NBC. When Katie joined the show, the number of viewers and the rating of the show skyrocketed.

In 2003, Couric guest-hosted The Tonight Show with Jay Leno as part of a swap campaign. She had 45% more viewers than Jay Leno.

Couric quickly moved up the ranks in the news industry and in 1991, she became the co-anchor of "The Today Show." Couric was an instant hit with viewers, who were able to easily relate to her blend of charm, compassion, and hard-hitting journalism.

By 1993, "Today" surpassed "Good Morning America" as the most-watched morning newsmagazine in the country, in large part due to Couric's popularity. She was so popular, in fact, that in 2002 she signed a contract with NBC for $65 million dollars over four and a half years, making her the world's highest-paid TV personality. She was the first woman to ever hold that title.

Couric made history yet again in 2006 when she debuted as the first female solo evening news anchor for CBS. As her success continued, *The Wall Street Journal* called Couric one of the most successful news anchors in history. Couric was smart, beautiful, and easy for viewers to relate to. She wanted to give people information and people wanted to listen.

Katie Couric's final move in her television career came in 2012, when she started her own talk show on ABC called "Katie." The show's debut was the most-watched premiere of daytime television since "Dr. Phil" aired in 2002. On the show, Katie tackles a wide range of issues that she feels her viewers can relate to. Not only are the issues relatable—Katie is as well. After her husband and sister both died tragically from cancer at early ages, Couric became one of

DID YOU KNOW...

Christiane Amanpour was one of the special correspondents on Katie Couric's show, "Katie."

Couric is the author of the best-selling book "The Best Advice I Ever Got: Lessons from Extraordinary Lives." Couric donates all the book's profits to Scholarship America.

the leading advocates for cancer research. She has founded and co-founded numerous cancer awareness and research organizations. She even displayed her own mammogram, a test for breast cancer, on national television to encourage women to go and get their own. Instead of hiding the pain of her husband's death, Couric used it as a way to promote the fight against cancer. She hoped that it would bring about better lives for other cancer victims and their families. Katie's reports are informative and emotional, allowing viewers to connect to her.

Katie has done a little bit of everything during her time as a television personality. She has worked in the field and at every major news network. She has hosted the Olympic Games, acted in movies, and even written top-selling books.

In 2014, Katie Couric made a big change. She left her television career and stepped in a new direction: online news. The internet is becoming a popular form of journalism, and Couric is ready to conquer it. In 2014, she joined the leagues of other online reports as the global news anchor for Yahoo.com. Katie Couric believes that the internet will be the journalism hotspot in the future, and she looks forward to making her mark there as well.

CHAPTER 5
CAUGHT IN THE WEB

Journalism on the web has already become a major contender for news. As more people look to the internet as their source of information, more online journalists are needed to cover the task (Katie Couric can't do it alone). These journalists are not all seasoned veterans. In fact, some, like Camryn Garrett, aren't even adults!

Camryn Garrett is an eighth-grader at Bay Shore Middle School in

INK TO ELECTRONIC

Online journalism is quickly replacing written mediums as the most effective way to spread news stories.

Bay Shore, New York. Like other kids, she goes to school, does her chores, and spends time playing sports and hanging with her friends. However, Camryn also has an amazing hobby—Camryn is a reporter for the *Time for Kids* magazine.

Camryn is one of only 10 kids who are picked each year to report for *Time for Kids*. As a reporter, Camryn's articles are published in the magazine and as online articles for everyone to read. Just like her adult counterparts, Camryn researches articles, travels to important events, and interviews important people.

Her most exciting assignment happened in 2013, when Camryn travelled to New York for the premiere of Disney's "Frozen." Camryn was in a crowd of grown-up journalists on the same assignment for their publications. When Camryn talks about the event, she admits that she was nervous. However, she is also proud that she was

DID YOU KNOW...

Camryn has written four novels, but has yet to publish them.

DID YOU KNOW...

Camryn named her laptop "Walden." She uses it to write all of her articles and novels.

there—she felt like she was just as much a journalist as the rest of them. And, unlike most of the press in attendance, Camryn even got the chance to interview Kristen Bell, one of the stars!

Camryn's brief journalism career isn't just limited to *Times for Kids.* She is continuing to make a name for herself on the web. Most recently, Camryn received the chance to start her own column for *Huffington Post*—an online news publication. "It's the coolest thing," Garrett said when interviewed about her work. "I like to Google myself. Now, I have articles I can look at and show to people." Though Camryn hasn't even started high school, her future looks bright.

Camryn isn't sure if she wants to be a journalist forever. However, she does know that wherever she ends up, she wants to write: "I want to write and I want people to read my work." Camryn's career goals change daily—she wants to be a journalist, a screenwriter, a

AT THE FRONT OF FROZEN

Camryn was one of the few journalists to get a one-on-one interview with Kristen Bell (voice of Ana) at the premiere of the Disney movie Frozen.

young-adult novelist, and a psychiatrist.

While her final destination is unknown, one thing is certain—Camryn won't let barriers stand in her way. Online journalism has allowed her, and other female journalists, to pursue their dreams and make their voices heard. Though it is still a new field, it is one that many journalists believe will be the future of their industry.

The future for journalists in all fields is unclear.

BARRIER BREAKERS

The last generation of female journalists has proven that women have what it takes to succeed. It's now up to future generations to keep fighting for women's equality in the field of journalism.

However, one thing is certain. Women in journalism have made a name for themselves, and they are continuing to prove that they have what it takes to succeed. Thanks to the work of women like Marlene Sanders, the field of journalism has been opened to women everywhere. Women like Katie Couric have torn down barriers that once kept women from reaching their dreams. Now, it's up to the next generation to keep them down.

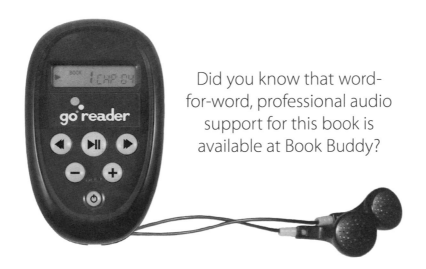

Did you know that word-for-word, professional audio support for this book is available at Book Buddy?

GoReader™ powered by Book Buddy is pre-loaded with word-for-word audio support to build strong readers and achieve Common Core standards.

The corresponding GoReader™ for this book can be found at: http://bookbuddyaudio.com

Or send an email to: info@bookbuddyaudio.com